Advance Praise

"I revel in the genius of simplicity," Laura Foley writes, as she gives us in plain-spoken but deeply lyrical moments, poems that explore a life filled with twists and turns and with many transformations. Through it all is a search for a fulfilling personal and sexual identity, a way to be most fully alive in the world. From multicultural love affairs, through marriage with a much older man, through raising a family, through grief, to lesbian love affairs, *Night Ringing* is the portrait of a woman willing to take risks to find her own best way. And she does this with grace and wisdom. As she says: "All my life I've been swimming, not drowning."

—**Patricia Fargnoli, author of** *Winter, Duties of the Spirit,* **and** *Then, Something*

I love the words and white space of poetry. I love stories even more. In this collection, Laura Foley evokes stories of crystallized moments, of quiet and overpowering emotion, of bathtubs and lemon chicken. The author grows up on the pages, comes of age, and reconciles past with present. Almost. Try to put the book down between poems to savor each experience. Try, but it won't be easy.

—**Joni B. Cole, author of** *Toxic Feedback, Helping Writers Survive and Thrive*

Plain-spoken and spare, Laura Foley's poems in *Night Ringing* trace a life story through a series of brief scenes: separate, intense moments of perception, in which the speaker's focus is arrested, when a moment opens to reveal a glimpse of the larger whole. Memories of a powerful, enigmatic father, a loving but elusive mother, a much older husband, thread Foley's stories of childhood, marriage and motherhood, finally yielding to the pressure of her attention, as she constructs a series of escapes from family expectations, and moves toward a new life. In these lucid, intense poems, Foley's quiet gaze, her concentration, and emotional accuracy of detail, render this collection real as rain.

—Cynthia Huntington, author of *Heavenly Bodies*

Foley's voice rings with quiet authority undercut by calamity, examining a life so extraordinary, she seems to have lived several people's lives, setting a high bar for poetic craft she meets, in great mystery perfectly expressed in the tiny, quotidian, "spent matches pressed on wet pavement," to soulful beauty, "as wind lifts/every shining wave"; in wisdom rooted in humor, from the deliciously funny "Flunking Jung," to self-deprecating wit, misreading "poetic" as "pathetic," reminding us wisdom is love, grown from self-compassion.

—April Ossmann, author of *Anxious Music*

Other Books by Laura Foley

Syringa

Mapping the Fourth Dimension

The Glass Tree

Joy Street

Night Ringing

Night Ringing

Laura Foley

HEADMISTRESS PRESS

Copyright © 2016 by Laura Foley.
All rights reserved.

ISBN-13: 978-0692585955
ISBN-10: 0692585958

This book may not be reproduced, in whole or in part, including illustrations, in any form (beyond that permitted by Sections 107 and 108 of the U.S. Copyright Law and except by reviewers for the public press), without written permission from the publishers.

Cover art © 2010 by Laura Foley, "Lightning Over Mt. Ascutney."
Cover & book design by Mary Meriam.

PUBLISHER
Headmistress Press
60 Shipview Lane
Sequim, WA 98382
Telephone: 917-428-8312
Email: headmistresspress@gmail.com
Website: headmistresspress.blogspot.com

To Clara Giménez

"Clara, why don't I dream of you?"

from "Paula Becker to Clara Westhoff," Adrienne Rich

(recorded in my journal, three months before I met, or heard of, my future partner, Clara Giménez)

Contents

I.

Turtle	1
Missing in Action	2
Summer Waters	3
Every Wave	4
In the Honda Service Area	5
In Unison	6
WTF!	7
Will	8
The Runner	9
Done, and Undone	10
Perfectly Chilled	11
Oblivion	12
Equus, or First Night	13

II.

At the Abortion Clinic	17
Morocco	18
Cantilevered Fairy Tale	19
The Staff of Life	20
Second Marriage, or Lemon Chicken	21
Stefan's Heaven	22
Daddy's Girls	23
The Happy Apartment	24
Driving Route 95	25
Night Ringing	26
Dad's Last Night	27

III.

Holocaust	31
Farm Life	32
The Sounds Oblivion Makes	33
Leaving Him	34
The Best Day of My Life	35
The Giving Tree	36
Waking Up	37
Online Dating	38
Coffee Beans	39
My Father's Roses	40
Deep in the Woods	41

IV.

Sign Language	45
How I Lost Her	46
Like Shadows	47
I Go Down to the River	48
City Romance	49
Not a God	50
Cavafy	51
The Doctor Tells Me to Drink Lots of Water	52
Two Women	53
At the Doctor's Office	54
Lapping Over Us	55
Shopping	56
Dream	57
Unanswered Question	58
Flunking Jung	59
Means of Escape	60

V.

Incident in the Coffee Shop	63
Tuesday Night	64
4 AM	65
Paradox	66
The Psychic Basement	67
The Alligator	68
"Where There Is Rejoicing, There Should Be Trembling"	69
The Fast Course of a Relationship	70
The Best	71
Ode to My Feet	72
Not Drowning	73
My Own Hand	74
Acknowledgments	77
Dedications	79
Thanks	81
About the Author	83

I.

Turtle

I dreamt of one,
big leathery body
lifting from the ocean
like a bird, but of the earth,
solid, strong, six feet long,
astonishing as any human
born from the mystery of sea.

Missing in Action

Lying on Mother's bedroom carpet, one Sunday afternoon with nothing to do, Mother busy with a long hot bath, Father working long hours at the hospital, older sisters courting madness in other rooms—no one to notice I've slowed my soundless breathing to nearly none, nearly perfected playing dead.

Summer Waters

The August I was eight,
just before the divorce,
Mom would get into the wine each night,
staring beyond me into purgatory,
corners of her lips curving up, falling,
in a strange, rhythmic dance.

Then she'd scratch her face to sores,
cigarettes glowing in the semi-dark,
like warning lights, and I'd escape,
run to town to leap the highest bridge,
falling deep in summer waters—
it felt like flying.

Every Wave

This morning, as a friend
drinks the potion prepared
to end her life,

having deemed her body unlivable
after two years' struggle—
I leave my house and ride

a ferry slowly across a lake,
as wind lifts
every shining wave.

In the Honda Service Area

We're sitting knee-to-knee
while her car gets new brakes, mine new fluids,
she discusses hip replacement,
in warrior-like detail with a friend,
each slice to flesh, how skin is spread
from bone, the pain she's in, her plans when she gets home,
the miracle of titanium. I'm trying not to hear,
two foam plugs squeezed snugly in my ears,
head bent low over *The Iliad*. I'm at the part
where Achilles, known for ripping limbs,
breaking hips apart, rests angry in his tent,
saying he will not fight, not for shining pots of gold,
nor the seven dancing girls Agamemnon offers.
But, time and again, her new hips, titanium and strong as a god's,
break through the Bronze Age scene, her voice
a wave dissolving the Trojan beach.

In Unison

Years before she leaves my father,
before she's subsumed
by wine's delusion,
Mother's doing exercises,
Jack LaLanne in shades of grey.
Too young for school,
I lie beside her, absorbing
her body warmth,
her comforting fragrance,
allies on the carpet,
lifting our arms
toward incandescent light.

WTF!

My father's initials on our towels, and luggage too, William Thomas Foley, known as Bill Foley to his golf buddies, but Dr. Foley to most everyone else, we children trained to answer the phone like secretaries, *Dr. Foley's Residence,* to rush the door each evening, offering succor. He'd ring his name in Morse code, banging the doorbell hard so I sprang from my games. If I failed, he'd enter my room and tell me, with arched lips and brows, *You've missed an opportunity to please.* Oh, it was easy enough to fling open the door. The hard part was after, meeting his gaze.

Will

Overpowering his
desire to stay dry
with mine to swim,
my thighs'
insistent pressure
around his warm belly,
my horse and I,
over our heads
in summer water.

The Runner

The stout woman in the hospital bed
taps where her leg once was,
tapping, tapping for the hour she talks—
she traveled the country,
held baseball scholarships,
was a runner, built a sugar house,
a barn for her heifers—still tapping,
she's got a high threshold for pain—
still tapping—pajamas soaked
in sweat, pus drenching the bed—
tapping I hear as an SOS,
though she says she never cries.

Done, and Undone

My mom's painting the bathtub, covering the scars from its former family. After the divorce, she, my sister, and I've moved to a small apartment, three rooms fronting a dark airshaft we fear to peer too deeply into. We've left home, the cavernous parkside flat infused with Dad's cold elegance, dining room the size of Alaska. Mom smothers the old bathtub in our new apartment with bright enamel paint we'll abuse as badly. Mom, with her Winstons and red lipstick, taking college courses she'll never finish, painting and repainting the tub, every year we live here.

Perfectly Chilled

The storm's a blizzard and Dad
calls me at Mom's to ask
if I think we should go.
I'm twelve, it's Christmas vacation,
so I say *Yes,* and we ride the slippery highway,
snow obliterating vision,
police closing the road behind us.
When he stops to call ahead,
his head is all we see
in the buried phone booth,
but the snow gods are on our side—
at the hotel, we're the only guests,
Dad, his gorgeous Swiss lover,
my classmate-friend and I,
snow-bound waiters with nothing to do
but serve the four of us,
and I love it, the box lunches,
days alone with my friend
on the soft and empty ski slopes,
evenings playing Scrabble—
and New Year's with Dad,
his bottle of Champagne
on the window ledge disappearing,
dropping down a twelve-foot snowdrift,
Dad cursing, laughing, relaxed
as he never was with Mother,
retrieving his celebratory wine,
chilled to perfection.

Oblivion

Middle of nowhere on a long trip east,
Mother swerves to avoid, but hits
the goofy grey sheepdog loping into us,
bright fur haloing its face—
stomach-clenching thud,
older sister suddenly serious,
suddenly thoughtful of me:
If you don't stop,
Laurie will remember this
her whole life—
but Mom won't stop
in the midst of oblivion.

Equus, or First Night

A group of twelve
from a fancy high school,
on a birthday outing for one of us,
daughter of a slain Kennedy.
We sit together, watching a teenage boy
romping onstage like a horse,
my first sight of a naked man
we cap off with piña coladas
at Trader Vic's,
eluding Secret Service agents,
hailing taxis in the street—
I hop, buoyant, in my trusty sneakers,
among this loose group of friends,
harboring a secret crush
on one of them.
At his house, emboldened
by my first taste of rum,
or strangeness of the play,
or the famous company,
I reach for him, and
in the morning we
eat cereal with his mom,
while the bells of St. Thomas More
remind me it's Sunday,
and nothing has changed,
and everything has changed.

II.

At the Abortion Clinic

Days of nausea, vomiting once in an alley en route to work. In mid-July, I'm three months pregnant, a result of diaphragm malfunction or my crazy belief it would work from the bureau drawer. Today the city malfunctions too, blackout sapping fans, airless apartments and clinic. My parents, divorced, don't know. My boyfriend frightens me, wants us to keep this baby. *It's mine,* he insists. *I'm a teenager,* I plead. In the waiting room, I meet Carlita, and I laugh a little, the first time in weeks. *I crave mustard, mint ice cream, pickles, all together,* she giggles, as we wait for light.

Morocco

My disapproving family's gone
AWOL from my life, so we elope,
flying to Tangier for our Arab wedding.
At the airport, greeted with news
of his mother's sudden death,
he can't stop weeping.
Plunging us in sixty days of Muslim mourning,
his family compensates,
treats me to choicest bits of lamb and plum,
pushes them to my side of the communal plate,
prepares broth for me when I develop fever,
an ugly boil growing on my face.
Sleepless nights I ponder how I got here,
this foreigner asleep beside me.
Afternoons, evenings, I linger by a window,
savor the muezzin's call,
prayerful echoes in the dusty streets.

Cantilevered Fairy Tale

I.

In wide-brimmed hat, encircling cape, black hair to his shoulders, hunched back, Mustapha approaches me on Second Avenue, invites me to his studio. He tells me he's a Moroccan prince, describes the accident, body cast when he was six, sings to me in Arabic, soothing lyrics from the Koran, *Allahu Akbar, Insha Allah.*

II.

During Ramadan we fast, long hot days of August without sustenance, for reasons I half understand. Nights, we brew a special soup. Nothing I won't do, no hunger I won't suffer, to save him.

III.

In my father's huge apartment building, we're relegated to the basement, a mine-like chamber adjacent to the boiler. My hunchback husband and I, sequestered dwarf-like in a hot shoebox room, sole window where I sit dreaming escape—a window barred to passing feet.

The Staff of Life

for Gary

They were strolling
a boulevard, hand
in hand, past an aromatic
Chinese restaurant,
simmering night of 'sixty-nine,
just home from Viet Nam—
when something inside him
broke, and he woke to find
his fingers locked
around his girlfriend's neck.
Forty years later, he's still in prison,
rising each day at 4 AM,
kneading softness into every fold,
punching down the risen dough,
baking the staff of life
for those who've given offense.

Second Marriage, or Lemon Chicken

It begins at the Chinese place
on Spring Street,
our first date.
Though the dish looks good,
I cannot eat.
He scrapes my leftovers
to the sidewalk
for his patient old Lab,
waiting by the restaurant door.
I have that queasy, excited feeling,
when you know something
is about to happen.

Stefan's Heaven

I visit him in his attic loft, *Stairs straight to Heaven,* he says. I like
the firmness of his step, boots, jeans, tweed Italian cap, Polish lilt,
his barely escaping the Holocaust, his dog, content beneath his desk.
He serves Cognac in little glasses, regales me with stories of Kabul,
his Fulbright in Afghanistan, mountain women with their chiseled
legs, illiterate men singing poems on the street, while sweeping. Soon
he's taking off my shirt, we're falling into bed. Wakeful as he sleeps, I
browse his desk: glasses, books, papers, an old bronze reading lamp,
an I.D. card, his birth date—not forty, as I thought he said, but
sixty—and I think: *I'm twenty-three and he's almost dead.* Tired at last,
I return to Heaven as he sees it, sleep like the dead.

Daddy's Girls

He wanted a boy so badly,
he called four girls
a Chinese curse,
blamed our mother,
haunted us, his
unwanted daughters.
Kiss me, he'd insist.
Quickly, we learned
to turn away,
duck his gaze,
but still he broke us:
two to madness,
one to meanness,
one to poetry.

The Happy Apartment

Seven floors above Broadway,
above the ice cream shop,
seven flights of stairs
I descend pregnant, each evening,
for my fresh-dipped
coffee-almond ice cream bar,
then climb back home.
Seven for exercise,
for the lucky number.
Seven stories soaring over the avenue.
More than seven large windows
over a leafy green campus,
St. John the Divine
gold in the morning light.
Three of us in two narrow rooms,
my desk in the corridor,
books towered everywhere,
our young dog's nursery
a closet in the hall,
where she gives birth to six
beautiful long-haired mutts;
and I in the bed,
a second blond boy.

Driving Route 95

We drive south, twenty-one hours straight,
to our ramshackle third home
we rent out for tax money,
keeping an attic room for the two of us,
then three, four, then five,
as our family expands—
and one year, thanks to our pregnant Lab,
we return north with eleven new pups.
But this story isn't about the dogs,
house, or bike rides to the beach,
manatees, dolphins or flying fish
lifting from the azure bay.
It's about the long drive south,
one year when our children are little,
two sons sleeping as Stefan drives,
me nursing the baby in the back,
drowsy, middle of the night.
When he stops for gas, goes inside,
I wake, place the baby in her car seat,
crawl over her, two sleeping sons, dogs,
to the restroom, emerging five minutes later
to the anonymous service station almost empty,
a cool, dark Carolina night,
where I see no van, no kids,
no dogs, no baby, no husband.
I'm alone on a moonless night,
far from home in the sleeping south.
My breasts and throat fill
with an ache I've never known,
that years later will become habitual.
But now, on this soft November night,
I'm a young mother whose whole family
is speeding away, unaware.
I commandeer an elderly couple
to rush me along the Interstate
till we see my van ahead, packed with life,
my life, for which we honk and wave.

Night Ringing

My dad's voice on the phone in the middle of the night, delivering the impossible-to-assimilate news of my little sister's death, in an Air Ambulance from botulism, after eating a bagel and cream cheese. *Don't let this spoil your milk,* he warns, my newborn baby asleep beside me. Three months later, I'm woken again, by ringing at 3 AM, this time my aunt's voice, *Your father...heart attack.* Now in Indonesia, half a world away from my ailing mom, jolted awake by insistent ringing, I'm stumbling through the dark, winding down a circular stair, to the place where the ringing doesn't end.

Dad's Last Night

He held my baby in his arms,
tossed tennis balls to my sons,
walked us three blocks to our car,
still so chilled, his cashmere coat
couldn't warm his blood
in the leaf-ridden wind.
Imagine then
his long walk home.

III.

Holocaust

I take our three children to the zoo,
leave my elderly husband
to enjoy hours of freedom
home alone.
When we return,
loud with our pleasure,
he sits, unmoving,
his afternoon spent staring
through time,
seeking his sister,
lost in Poland
over forty years ago.

Farm Life

My thighs itch from the rattling machine,
rusted iron seat and flying hay,
Stefan driving the four-by-four,
pulling me, mostly willingly,
rat-a-tat-tat of blades on grass,
as I watch for stones,
ready to holler if I see one,
and once, the cutter hitting a rock I don't see—
airborne for a moment,
over hay laid to rest in rows,
a brief, foreboding view.

The Sounds Oblivion Makes

We're in the barn,
my job to pour gasoline
into the carburetor
of the old Toyota wagon,
as he cranks the key repeatedly,
and when the can ignites—
burns my lashes, eyebrows—
I drop it, flaming, onto dry hay,
and for a panicked interim
we run back and forth,
moan and yelp like animals,
as we fill buckets from the horse trough,
dump water on flames,
fire lapping the barn walls,
cackling with greedy glee,
and my little sister, on a weekend visit,
oblivious on the lawn watching us,
pets the purring cat.

Leaving Him

Early April.
Soft rain.
Spring
about to begin.

The Best Day of My Life

It's unseasonably hot, and I'm alone in my new house, without a fan. I've reclaimed my name, dropped my husband's, moved away from him and the house where our children were born, house I don't own—no version of my name on the deed. House we expanded, gardens we tended, attic room where we slept, fields we mowed, all his. Alone in my new house with my name on the deed, not my husband's, just mine. Alone for the first evening, our children with him overnight. This record-setting June, I drive my new road to buy a fan. No one knows where I am.

The Giving Tree

Out for an early morning walk,
past cornfields bare this day in March,
I pass a stand of maple trees,
iron spigots stuck out like lips,
sap buckets so full, they're dripping over.
No one's around. I straighten
a metal bucket, make a pond of hands,
catching clear, cold liquid in them.
Lap cat-like, the sweetness of a giving tree.

Waking Up

Between adolescence
and menopause,
I limited my writing
to logging weather.
Turtle-like, my emotions
and intellect dug in deep
beneath frozen ponds.
I saw one yesterday,
mud caked on her back,
stunned by April light,
remembering how
to breathe before
her next big steps:
find another mate,
lay eggs, bury them.
Remember
how to snap.

Online Dating

He's the good-looking
grey-haired guy,
Bronxville widower,

a photographer, intelligent face
wooing me
from my monitor.

We arrange a call. He entertains me
with his complete medical history,
weak heart, broken ankle,

enlarged prostate, confides
he pees in a bag.
His late wife?

Oh, last year,
she locked me out of the house,
tore everything up,

called the cops,
killed herself. Now,
tell me something about you...

Coffee Beans

CoffeebeansintothehopperCoffee
beansintothehopperCoffeebeans
intothehopper—Sometimes
this sound is enough,
when your sister tells you
she likes Enron, supports Rehnquist,
Reagan, J.P. Morgan, both Bush presidents,
many other famous Texans—Coffeebeansinto
thehopperCoffeebeansintothe
hopperCoffeebeans
intothehopper
Coffee
beans
into
the
hopper
Coffeebeansintothehopper—
sweet as rain.

My Father's Roses

I'm annoyed,
passing my father's roses
every day,
as I walk to work—
flagrant colors, clamoring
years past his death,
outside his old office
on York.
How I hated
how attentive
he was to them,
lacing their stems
with pesticides,
reciting the names
of every damn one,
clipping their skinny necks,
manicured fingers
tenderly placing each
in its own vase,
never minding their thorns.

Deep in the Woods

My friend and I
lean over a stream,
looking for the moose
she saw here once,
ancient beast
at the curve
where the woods
grow dark. Our hands
almost touch.
The brook below us
swirls with foam,
filling the silence
between us.

IV.

Sign Language

Post-stroke,
my mother's last speech
voiced no words,
but I heard them
in her gesture to us,
*My darling ones, my
babies,* motion of tears
as her train disappeared.

How I Lost Her

Mother didn't die
of the stroke which left
her mute, didn't die
in Chuck's Steak House,
where she ate
with a friend
that night.

It was later, when,
alone in her room,
a bit of leftover meat
stuck in her throat—
and she didn't press
the red bell
by her bed, couldn't

call out, staggering
into the hallway,
falling where they
found her
hours later.

Like Shadows

I call my youngest child,
institutionalized for six years, home.

I call her home to sleep
in a room her own again,

no return to "school" possible.

I spend two hours alone,
before she wakes,

two hours of quiet
at my kitchen table,

not enough hours, looking out
at the autumn fog

as birds like shadows
pass by mine.

I Go Down to the River

After making love with a woman
for the first time ever,
I go down to the river where I grew up
and touch it, for the first time ever,
dipping my fingers in the chill East River,
tasting salt from the sea,
as boat-waves flow toward me,
washing over my ankles,
as black-tipped seagulls circle my head.

City Romance

Because I think I'm in love,
I go out at night to see the snow,
how it falls and vanishes in the river
and know she is seeing it too,
who lives not far from here,
somewhere there
on the opposite shore.

Because she thinks she's in love,
she's made a plan to walk
across the Williamsburg Bridge
in the storm tomorrow,
to meet me above the river,
so we can be together
over the water, in the snow.

Not a God

I realize, now, my analyst is a person.
Is separate from myself.
No righteous lightning bolts
or magical revelations.

Alone with the one
least visible of gods,
and out the window,
all those stones of winter.

Cavafy

So much work awaits,
my small room littered with books,
half-written papers, mid-unit
evaluations, applications, essays.

Still I go out,
sit in the coffee shop all day
reading Cavafy's poems,
lost like him
to all but the sensuous life.

I cross slippery streets,
slide down two avenues
through icy tunnels,
under low-leaning branches,
to reach the old Greek coffee shop.

The great gay poet
wrote of his shame, his
strong desire for men,
could have been killed
for his love.

My window seat
offers a view out—or in—
as ice drops
from the roiled heavens.

The Doctor Tells Me to Drink Lots of Water

Finding myself aflutter, dizzy,
faint, I rush to the doctor.
She draws blood from my vein,
straps me to an EKG machine,
stares into my eyes,
tells me I'm fine.
Your heart's normal, she says.
For a fire, I say.

Two Women

We meet on the boardwalk,
biggest moon of the year
lifting her pretty face
from the river to the east,
savor sweet mangoes
we buy on the street.
Dripping, soft and ripe,
we eat by moonlight,
without a knife.

At the Doctor's Office

When the doctor says
I have permanent
hearing loss in both ears,

I imagine a monarch,
wide wings propped
on fragile legs,
resting on the wise doctor's
balding head.

I shiver in their
thin green gown,
completely fit, except
this constant ringing
I've heard for years,

a side effect, I thought,
of silent retreats,
a hyper-attunement attained
through much hard work,

a sensitivity to the movement
of my body's cells,
my inner cricket's
tic, tic, tic.

When he adds:
It will get worse—
the butterfly lifts
on able wings
from its slippery perch,
unimpeded by dangling legs.

Lapping Over Us

I walk around the busy block, inundated with sense impressions, spent matches pressed on wet pavement, wind whistling roofs, a weary beggar leaning on a cane. All day I've sat and written almost nothing, just one sentence, a truth, about his penis. All day I've been reading of aesthetics and the unconscious, dreams and the will. Last night I dreamt of cats standing, two-legged on a beach, forepaws cuffed behind backs. How shall we make sense of these images, lapping over us, day and night, or the sense in a sentence? *He could still hang a towel on it, erect, when he was eighty-three.*

Shopping

When I go shopping
for tee shirts, pants, a coat,
I'm embarrassed by sales clerks,
dressing room attendants, shoppers,
who might steal a look at me
as I study my mirror self.
Even groceries make me shy.
*Do I recognize my former therapist
in the dairy aisle?*
So, when my new lover proposes
we visit a sex shop together,
it's so scary, so outrageous,
I just say *Yes*.

Dream

In my dreams, he's still annoying,
lying fully clothed next to me,
whispering too loudly.
I know he'll disturb the baby,
who nurses a cat beneath the bed,
unless I leave.
I'm sure he won't mind or even notice,
he's that dumb and senile.
My mom plays with a kitten
on the bed in the other room.
I'm happy to leave that silly house,
leap some fences.
Too bad I forgot to put on pants.

Unanswered Question

She crosses the bay to meet me,
copper hair shining,
bike flying down
the ferry's gangway.
I'm so happy, my feet tingle
as we pedal to the beach.
We swim in the placid sea,
do backbends in the sand.
She reads to me,
eats a chocolate cherry,
slips another from her mouth
to mine.
When her mood changes,
a sinkhole opens under us.
She tightens her fists,
pulling me by the wrists,
while near us,
two seagulls dance
on twig feet, squawking,
beaks locked,
and I don't know
if it's love or violence.

Flunking Jung

Ten-fifteen, in pajamas, the night before the Jungian entrance exam, I'm startled by shrieking from the basement, red box I've never noticed, flashing red and yellow lights, TANK ALARM. Oh, great. Pull a switch, silence the shriek, ignore the impending mess. The next day, one hand on the steering wheel, one on the phone, I'm calling septic companies, driving the Interstate to Boston, where my examiners ask for a recent dream. I tell one about an awkward dentist who drops a filling in a floor-crack, as I watch from a bus. *We don't like this dream,* they snap, *you weren't driving the bus,* and flunk me. I should've told them about the septic tank exploding, filling my basement with shit—a dream with plenty of fodder for thought. The next day, a young fox visits my garden, serene gold eyes, a Jungian gift, redeeming the flunk.

Means of Escape

She runs after me, pleading
I love you, I need you,
come back, let's talk more.
But I'm out the door—
we've been talking all night.
She follows me barefoot,
shrieks like a harlot,
alerts the whole block:
You're a fucking bitch!
I pause, struck
by the sight of her toes,
aquamarine-painted moons
pressed against pavement,
as I trace in my mind
every crack in the old concrete.
When I look up again,
into the lines of a face
I once thought pretty,
I'm suddenly happy,
suddenly free.

V.

Incident in the Coffee Shop

I'm having my usual,
OJ, bialy, eggs poached easy.
I've known this waitress years:
Florence has met my kids,
my sons' girlfriends,
my lover who I'm
breaking up with.
Today, when she asks
if everything's okay,
I begin to cry,
before realizing
she means the food.

Tuesday Night

Finally, I threaten to call the police
or the hospital, then drive off
with the dog
so she'll see I'm serious,
though it enlightens neither of us—
packing the whining puppy in back,
my daughter yelling from the porch,
me driving one-half mile to town,
filling my empty gas tank,
returning home. She's changed
into her light blue dog pajamas,
no longer rebellious, but scared
of doctors and police,
and I'm still rigid,
still angry in my dead-calm way,
and she's whimpering for a hug,
her face red and sad
and deeply uncomprehending—
upwelling in my chest a thawing
tenderness for this teenage child.

4 AM

This morning, I wake
to cracking ice,
freezing rain and sleet
sliding from the roof,
pounding down,
night wanting in.
I'm supposed to get up,
ride coach to New York.
All night, wind rattled
these old wooden walls.
I leave the cold
where it belongs,
roll over in bed,
pull blankets up to my chin,
turn stillness in.

Paradox

A friend writes that my *poetic words*
fill her with strength, but I read
pathetic, which is exactly
what I'm feeling, a familiar ache,
a longing for someone
to write to me, my ex-beloved,
who *doesn't want to resume contact,*
who I know for a million reasons I don't wish
to resume contact with either, who
I foolishly wish to see—
sitting in the sun's gold slant
without seeing it, thinking
maybe I'll surprise her in New York,
sit on the sidewalk with my dog,
in the cold, of course,
holding a handmade sign, *Marry Me.*

The Psychic Basement

Boston is too hot, overcrowded, overdeveloped, too many cars—maybe Nietzsche's right about apocalypse. Even in the brick basement, site of a Jungian conference, eight of us nearly faint. On a break, we meet outside in hundred-degree heat. *This airlessness must be psychic,* one says. *Or the lack of air conditioning,* I snap. *I'm falling asleep,* says another. The banal speaker lectures on and on about Jung's sad love affairs with clients Spielrein and Wolff, taking greatness down a notch—maybe that's why I feel sick. Happily, I have to leave early, for Nina's birthday. *Look at the piglets, Mommy, nine babies. Don't go close to the sow, she'll kill you,* she laughs, as we skirt the electric fence. *And here's the calf, I named her, Ginger Snap. Look how she sucks my wrist. Isn't she cute?* Away from the psychic basement, I revel in the genius of simplicity.

The Alligator

We rode a ferry,
my daughter and I,
across the river to meet
my Brooklyn lover,
who greeted us, shining
on her silver bicycle,
short hair flying.
At a café, we shared
an alligator burger,
reptile flesh,
split three ways,
Cajun-spiced,
barbequed just right.
No longer my lover,
I cannot forget her,
nor the alligator who
almost married us.

"Where There Is Rejoicing, There Should Be Trembling"

—Psalm 211

A fracture of no consequence,
this glass breaking in the heat
as my son is married.
Not the Jewish glass
wrapped in cloth and stomped on,
but a small pane cracking by chance
as the church window is opened
to welcome air,
all of us turning in our pews to look.

The Fast Course of a Relationship

Only last week, I brought her
a white magnolia snapped
from my front yard,
smelling like honey.

A country guest,
she accepted the blossom
with a kiss. I find it today,
without a trace of fragrance.

The Best

After our weekend together,
picnic on Governors Island,
double-decker tour bus,
Empire State Building,
Top of the Rock!,
my "developmentally disabled"
teenager texts me from the train:
sooo tierd but hade a nis tim
thx mom love uu.
I think of my friend's daughter,
an angry fifteen-year-old,
Red Bull-addicted,
recently caught shoplifting,
and text mine back:
Love you too, Babe.
You're the Best!
Each blade of grass
so green, under my feet.

Ode to My Feet

For years I've thought them queer,
hiding them
in steamy boots and sneakers,
but recently, I've begun to like
their well-worked lines, blue veins,
tapered, skinny elegance.
Funny-looking, yes, oddly
protuberant, awkwardly angled,
unlike anyone else's,
models for a medieval statue's,
ancient granite feet
on a church facade,
thoroughly unmodern.
Yet, how well they climb steep cliffs,
work my slinky kayak's rudder,
how they tingle, tapping to music
across a wooden floor,
dangling below me
when I sit on high seats,
and turning pink as we wade
the cool mountain pond,
warming, as they carry me
faithfully home to rest.

Not Drowning

On my back like a corpse, enjoying buoyancy,
I drift downstream as Amtrak, hooting, passes over.

I wave at passengers from the city,
peering down at me with concern.

All my life I've waved at passersby,
now I wave so they know I'm not dead.

All my life I've been swimming, not drowning,
despite any appearance to the contrary.

My Own Hand

It's a cappuccino
kind of day,
my way to medicate,
I've come to understand,
my own hand which lifts to me,
as if to say, *Darling*.

Acknowledgments

Thanks to the editors of the following publications where these poems first appeared, sometimes in earlier versions:

A Year of Being Here: "The Giving Tree"

Alexandria Quarterly: "Equus, or First Night"

Atlanta Review: "Driving Route 95"

Buddhist Poetry Review: "Every Wave"

Harpur Palate: "The Sounds Oblivion Makes," winner of the Milton Kessler Memorial Prize in Poetry

Lavender Review: "I Go Down to the River"

Mom Egg Review: "Like Shadows"

Pulse Magazine: "In the Honda Service Station"

Sinister Wisdom: "Deep in the Woods"

String Poet: "At the Doctor's Office"

The Gay & Lesbian Review: "Two Women"

The Good Men Project: "Lapping Over Us" and "Shopping"

Valparaiso Poetry Review: "My Father's Roses" and "Where There Is Rejoicing, There Should Be Trembling"

Women's Voices for Change: "Ode to My Feet" and "Summer Waters"

World Enough Writers, Ice Cream Poems Anthology: "The Happy Apartment"

Dedications

"Dad's Last Night," to William T. Foley, in memory.

"Deep in the Woods," to Peggy Madden.

"Driving Route 95," to Aaron, Billy and Nina Sharff.

"Holocaust," to Stefan Sharff, in memory.

"My Own Hand," to the baristas of Tuckerbox Café, White River Junction, VT.

"Night Ringing," to Alix Foley, in memory.

"Not a God," to Susan McKenzie.

"Sign Language," to Barbara Ball Cosden, in memory.

"The Happy Apartment," to Billy Sharff.

"The Psychic Basement" and "The Best," to Nina Sharff.

"The Staff of Life," to Gary, Northern NH Correctional Facility.

"Where There Is Rejoicing, There Should Be Trembling," to Aaron and Samantha Sharff.

Thanks

Thanks to my publishers, Mary Meriam, Risa Denenberg, and Rita Mae Reese, for their encouragement of my work and their vision of Headmistress Press; to my editor, April Ossmann, for her amazing skills; to Cynthia Huntington and Joni B. Cole, for their enthusiasm, writing workshops, guidance and inspiration; to my poet friends Carol, Anne, Clyde, Sue, Heather, and Pam, for the ongoing camaraderie and insights. Thank you to Mt. Ascutney and the Connecticut River, right out my window, keeping me company for all the years of solitude. Thank you to Clara Giménez, for coming into my life, awakening me from the night.

About the Author

Laura Foley is the author of four previous poetry collections, including *The Glass Tree,* which won the *Foreword* Book of the Year Award in Poetry (Silver), and *Joy Street,* which won the Bi-Writer's Award in Poetry.

Her poems have appeared in journals, magazines, and anthologies, including *Valparaiso Poetry Review, Aesthetica, Atlanta Review, Inquiring Mind, Pulse Magazine, Weatherings, Poetry Nook, Lavender Review, Mom Egg Review,* and many others.

She won *Harpur Palate's* Milton Kessler Memorial Prize in Poetry, the Grand Prize in *Atlanta Review's* International Poetry Contest, a poetry fellowship from Frost Place, and Columbia University's Bunner Prize for her work on Wallace Stevens. *Night Ringing* was a finalist for the Autumn House Poetry Prize.

Laura Foley holds graduate degrees in English Literature from Columbia University. Trained in chaplaincy through the New York Zen Center for Contemplative Care, she volunteers in hospitals and prisons, and is a certified Shri Yoga Instructor. She lives in the woody hills of Pomfret, Vermont with her partner Clara Giménez, and three big dogs.

Headmistress Press Books

Lovely - Lesléa Newman
Teeth & Teeth - Robin Reagler
How Distant the City - Freesia McKee
Shopgirls - Marissa Higgins
Riddle - Diane Fortney
When She Woke She Was an Open Field - Hilary Brown
God With Us - Amy Lauren
A Crown of Violets - Renée Vivien tr. Samantha Pious
Fireworks in the Graveyard - Joy Ladin
Social Dance - Carolyn Boll
The Force of Gratitude - Janice Gould
Spine - Sarah Caulfield
Diatribe from the Library - Farrell Greenwald Brenner
Blind Girl Grunt - Constance Merritt
Acid and Tender - Jen Rouse
Beautiful Machinery - Wendy DeGroat
Odd Mercy - Gail Thomas
The Great Scissor Hunt - Jessica K. Hylton
A Bracelet of Honeybees - Lynn Strongin
Whirlwind @ Lesbos - Risa Denenberg
The Body's Alphabet - Ann Tweedy
First name Barbie last name Doll - Maureen Bocka
Heaven to Me - Abe Louise Young
Sticky - Carter Steinmann
Tiger Laughs When You Push - Ruth Lehrer
Night Ringing - Laura Foley
Paper Cranes - Dinah Dietrich
On Loving a Saudi Girl - Carina Yun
The Burn Poems - Lynn Strongin
I Carry My Mother - Lesléa Newman
Distant Music - Joan Annsfire
The Awful Suicidal Swans - Flower Conroy
Joy Street - Laura Foley
Chiaroscuro Kisses - G.L. Morrison
The Lillian Trilogy - Mary Meriam
Lady of the Moon - Amy Lowell, Lillian Faderman, Mary Meriam
Irresistible Sonnets - ed. Mary Meriam
Lavender Review - ed. Mary Meriam

www.ingramcontent.com/pod-product-compliance
Lightning Source LLC
Chambersburg PA
CBHW071234090426
42736CB00014B/3071